Through Her Eyes

Yasmin Awan

Presentation by *BookLeaf Publishing*

Web: www.bookleafpub.com

E-mail: info@bookleafpub.com

ISBN : 9789358365634

First edition 2022

For my parents Shanila and Tahir.

For all you gave me. For all you
continue to give. I love you.

xXx

PREFACE

A peek through the window into how I
see the world.

1.

Where Did it Go?

When people ask me - where did it go?

I shake my head and tell them I really don't know.

Because I'm sure I had it right there in my hands,

But it trickled straight through my fingers like sand.

First it was there and then it was gone,

I used to have so much, now it feels like I have none.

I wish I'd taken more care of it and cherished it truly,

Who could have guessed life could treat us so cruelly?

I did have it once. I did. Didn't I?

Endless amounts from the ground to the sky.

But then it slipped away before I ever even knew,

I should have listened when they told me it flew.

I realise now that it was never truly mine,

Or anyone else's for that matter, because no one can hold time.

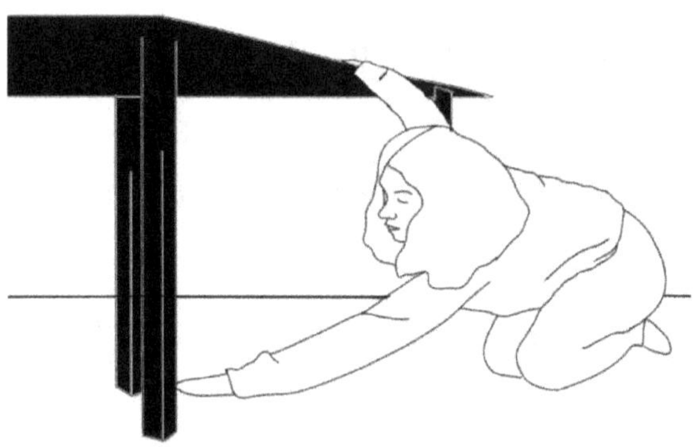

2.

The Escape Artist

He's running away, his cheeks a furious cherry,

Like when Santa Claus has been on the sherry,

He's panting now and breathing hard,

As he races over through the yard,

Determination burns in his bright blue eyes,

And the ache sets in, in his calves and his thighs,

Come on now, he's almost there!

Wind whips through his dirty blonde hair,

But, alas, he was never going to make it,

Because, this woman he could never truly outwit,

So as he huffs and clenches his fists,

She runs up behind him and pulls him
up by the wrist,

He kicks and flails and thrashes his legs
in the air,

If he knew the words, he'd probably
swear,

But he doesn't, so he just babbles
looking glum,

And holds hands tight, trailing after
mum.

3.

Aqua de Vida

The water brings me silence.

The water brings me peace.

The water stills my beating heart and brings my pulse to cease,

The water drowns my sorrows, the water eases my pain,

The water makes my spirit soar like I was dancing in the rain,

The water takes my voice, the water helps me breathe,

And I know my heart belongs to all the seven seas,

I feel my screaming lungs that were born of the shore,

And the last thing I remember, is to hear the ocean roar.

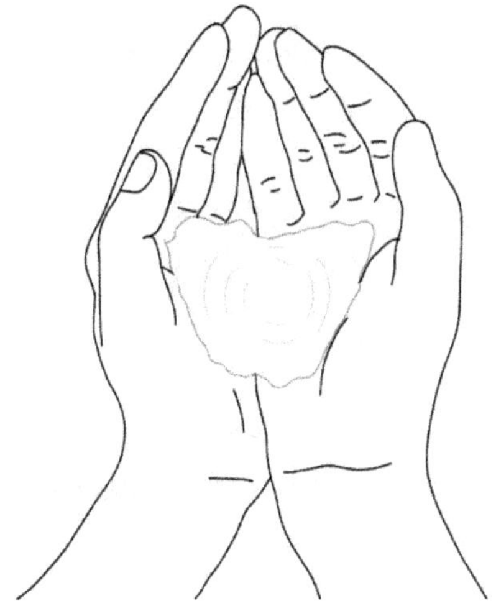

4.

Coastal Dream

And with the sun setting lower, down
into the sky,

My head held up and my face held high,

I breathe in the tang of salt sea air,

As it clings to my skin and leaves a
crunch in my hair,

I can taste it on my tongue and the smell
fills my nose,

Taking it all in from my head to my toes,

The crystal clarity of sapphire waters
enough to make any artist weep,

The sparkling glitter of sunshine off the
ocean waves make me sigh in defeat,

For my heart is lost to me, taken by
another,

Along with my spirit and my soul to the
great sea mother,

The ocean holds my heart and it holds
my soul,

I was captured by her staggering beauty,
more perfect than any stories told,

She is elegance and perfection, she is
beauty and grace,

You can see my adoration from the look
on my face,

She is as clear as glass, she is light as
the sunup high,

She is cloudy as a rainstorm, she is dark
as the night sky,

Waves lapping at the shore, she
breathes deep and slow,

Turmoil on the surface, but pure calm
and stillness in the depths down below.

5.

Daydreamer

Girl in the park, legs in the air,

Laid on her tummy, laughing without
care,

Runs her fingers across the pages of an
old tattered book,

Of all the pristine covers it was this one
that she took -the classic that she's read
time and time again,

Maybe a hundred times, even one
hundred and ten,

She loves to get lost in someone else's
world,

Gentlemen in top hats and tailcoats and
ladies in pearls,

Absorbed in this story, she runs her toes
through the grass,

Oblivious to families, couples and
children as they pass,

The sun gently browning her shoulders
and her back,

Her face just shaded by her flowered
sunhat,

Rays of shine turn strands of brown hair
to gold,

A smile on her lips as the story unfolds,

As she reaches the end she breathes a
happy sigh,

And rolls onto her back to look up at the
sky,

She stretches and yawns and lazily
rises to her feet,

Picks up her book, still barefoot and
turns to saunter home down the street.

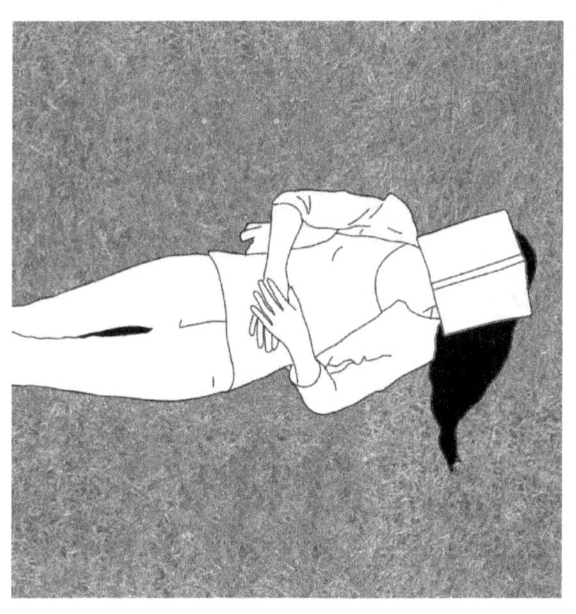

6.

Tidal

Waves are peaceful, waves are calm,

They are the familiar lines upon my
palm,

Waves are tidal, waves are great,

Can bring about more destruction than
any earthquake,

Waves are beauty, waves are grace,

They are the constant through time and
space,

Waves will lap lazily upon the shore

As it has done forever, as it will do
forever more.

7.

Bright

Turn your face towards the sun, fill your day with laughter and fun,

And soon the shadows will fall behind,

And all the darkness will leave your mind,

The future ahead is so very bright,

Filled with love and filled with light,

Go forth with passion, go forth with heart,

For this is a clean and brand new start,

Feel that excitement bubble down in your belly,

That makes your heart beat fast and your knees like jelly,

Breathe out the old and breathe in the new,

Those negative thoughts are done and through,

Pain and hardships will fade away,

Now these happier times are here to stay.

8.

Aqua Pura

Drown my sorrows, drown my pain,

Soothe my mind when I'm going insane,

Touch my lips, quench my thirst,

Even if you're starving, no water would kill you first,

Sapphire blue, emerald green, crystal clear, aquamarine,

Clear elixir that brings life, sustains us all,

Waves like lungs of the sea, rise and fall,

Breathing of the ocean, as waves lap the shore,

As they have done in history and will do forevermore.

9.

Balance

I am fire and I am ice,

The sugary sweetness, the heat and spice,

I am hard like a diamond but soft as the rain,

I have been invincible and still cried out in pain,

I am a hurricane that will tear across the sea,

I am the gentle breeze that lifts the petals and the leaves,

I am the earth and the dirt and the mud,

I am the crystal water, the purity, the flood,

I am the darkest black that makes you scared of the night,

I am the most dazzling light that makes
your days so bright,

I am the widest smile laughing in the
face of fears,

I am the shattered and broken, drowning
in her tears,

I am not one, and I am not the other, this
you can clearly see,

Both live within, these are the two sides
of me.

10.

Lost

For those moments that you're not so sure,

When decisions are hard but your intentions are pure,

For those times when you are filled with doubt,

And all you want to do is shut it all out,

When you try and listen to the voice of reason,

But you're not quite sure and you change your mind like seasons,

When you don't know which direction to turn,

It's ok, because from every mistake you'll learn,

You'll grow and develop and make yourself better,

Spell it out if you have to, letter by letter,

You're allowed to get it wrong
sometimes, You're allowed to make
mistakes,

No-one in the world gets it right all the
time, remember that for all our sakes,

Do what feels best by you, do what feels
right inside,

And even if things don't work out, at
least you know you tried.

11.

Best Friends

Hair EVERYWHERE! The house is such
a mess!

Sometimes it feels like this is just an
extra stress,

The early morning yawns and the sighs
late at night,

But no matter the time of day you
always greet me with delight,

You bound around and give me that
loony goofy grin,

You don't contain your excitement and
you headbutt me on the chin,

And I'm dazed for a moment but then I
start to laugh,

Because I love you for it, even though
you're so daft!

You're a softie for affection and you
adore giving hugs,

And it fills my heart with joy because I
know it's unconditional love,

You look at me with those big brown
eyes and I'm sure you understand,

I ruffle your ears and smile at you and
you lean your head into my hand,

And I know I moan about the early starts
and the walks in rain or snow,

And roll my eyes when you refuse to
fetch after a particularly far away throw,

Through all the holey socks and chewed
up skirting board,

And the millions of broken toys that you
for some reason love to hoard,

I take one look at you, at your dopey
lovely face,

And know that in my heart you hold a
very special place, I know exactly why
they say it, you truly are man's best
friend,

I love you, dopey doggie from the beginning until the worlds end.

12.

Blessed

Sometimes I forget how lucky I am,

All my life since I was a tot in a pram,

I've wanted for nothing and been so very blessed,

My family worked so hard to provide for me the best,

I have food on my table and a roof over my head,

I can rest easy at night in a clean comfy bed,

And sometimes I moan about inconveniences so small,

When in the grand scheme of things, they don't matter at all,

I have never been profoundly hungry, I have never known true pain,

But I whinge when I'm at work and put
under the slightest strain,

I would do well to remember, to remind
myself every day,

To be grateful, to be thankful that I have
things that for some people pray.

13.

Paradise

The sun, the sea, the heat, the sand,

My favourite place in all the land,

The place where I can truly be me,

The place I forever long to be,

To feel the sunshine beat down on my
shoulder,

I want to stay here forever, as I get
older,

To be in the place that makes me smile,

To remain here for the longest while,

To watch the sun set and rise,

Over the sea into the skies,

To feel the water run over my skin,

As the waves roll over and the tide
comes in,

To feel the soft sand in-between my
toes,

As I close my eyes and wiggle my nose,

And I smell the salt-tinged twang of the
ocean,

And listen to the waves with their soft
rolling motion,

Lazily lapping upon the shore,

Pulling away the sand, with each time a
little more,

To gaze at the windmills as they keep
turning way up high,

Where in the distance the mountains
touch the sky,

I could stand here all day from dawn to
dusk,

From the early morning crispness to the
evening soft musk,

I could watch the colours entwining in
the water, sapphire blues and emerald
greens,

Turn from turquoise to inky black as the
day turns dark, taken over by the night
queen,

Where over the water lights are
shimmering,

Reflected in the Aegean dancing and
glimmering,

To have the soles of my feet feel the
coolness of the sand,

And the wind in my hair and a rose in
my hand,

To hear the murmurings of fisherman
comparing their catches on the pier,

And watch the small fish in the shallows
of the water so clear,

But then I breathe a sigh, heavy and
deep,

And I open my eyes as I awake from the most perfect sleep.

14.

Sweet Tooth

I just can't help it, I really can't I swear,

I have zero will power when they're just
lying there,

Sat on the counter top just waiting for me,

My eyes light up and I smile with glee,

Sherbet and lollypops and Turkish delight,

Choux buns and chocolate eclairs begging
for a bite,

Cookie dough and brownies and pancakes
galore,

Waffles and crepes and biscuits and
s'mores,

The sweetest sweet tooth you've ever
known,

Sugar queen sat on her throne,

Don't leave temptation out, no you mustn't
do that,

Because it won't be there by the time you get back.

15.

Rain

I like the sound of thunder and rain,

As I sit and watch it hit the window pane,

The flashes of lightning that fire up the sky,

Grateful that I'm inside, safe, warm and dry,

Wrapped up in a blanket with a mug of hot chocolate and cream,

Huddled up, warming my fingers and inhaling the steam,

Pattering of raindrops muffled by the roof,

Sat next to a bowl of sticky toffee to satiate my sweet tooth,

Occasionally, I like to feel the rain dancing on my skin,

But more often than not, I'd rather watch it from within,

I like the sound of rain, when I can watch from the inside out,

Not a fan of being left out in it for too long, of that have no doubt,

I like the ripples it makes on the surface of the pond,

And the jewels of crystal drops that cling to leaves and fronds,

You can almost hear the greenery laughing in delight,

The rain quenches their thirst, keeps them healthy and sprite,

A perfect cycle, an everyday miracle, liquid gold that falls from the sky,

Purer than the salty tears that escape from sad eyes,

I like the sound of thunder and I like the sound of rain,

But I also like to remember that the sun will shine again.

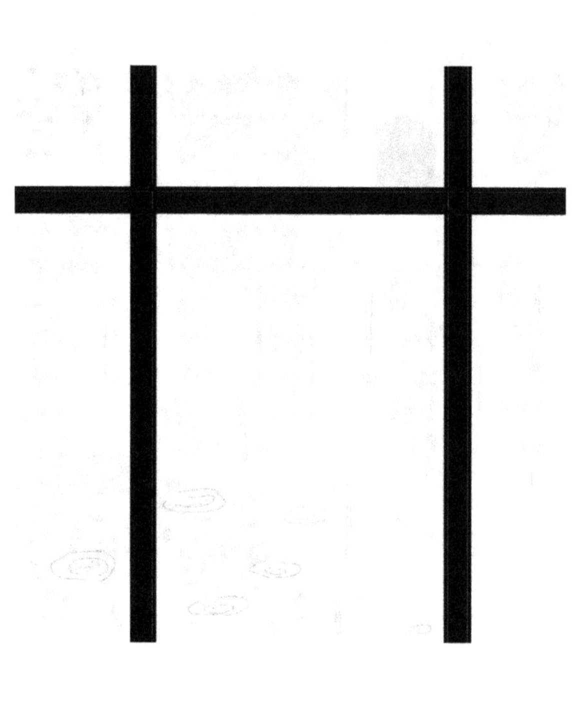

16.

Safari

I sit quiet, out of sight and out of mind,

As I watch them all, different types and different kinds,

They come and they go,

The neverending ebb and flow,

With their different voices and different noises,

Making different decisions and different choices,

So far apart from each other, the way they walk, the way they move,

Some that don't care, some with everything to prove,

Some with voices high, some low and deep,

Some bright eyed and some still half asleep,

On the prowl up in the sticks,

Ready for their early morning fix,

Looking sharp and tailored or slouchy
and chill,

Neither wants to leave until they get
their fill,

Grunts and gruffs and snorts and sniffs,

Some come alive when they just get a
whiff,

What will it be? One shot? Two shots?

I stop listening and go back to my book
in the corner of the coffee shop.

17.

The Willow Tree

It's cool but pleasant under the shade,

Sitting in the flowers of the grassy green glade,

Hear the leaves sigh as they dance in the breeze,

Watch the purple flowers be kissed by the bees,

To the north yellow fields as far as the eye can see,

While you sit underneath your favourite willow tree,

With your back against the bark and your knees up to your chest,

Here you are a visitor, Mother Nature's guest,

Close your eyes and listen to the sounds of the earth,

Feel the breeze in your hair and your toes in the dirt,

Hear the sparrows sing and the bees hum their song,

In this place you find your peace and desire to stay all day long,

The floral hints that carry in the air,

Lifts the tendrils on your shoulders as it plays with your hair,

And you smile to yourself as you take it all in,

For nature truly is the most beautiful thing,

You lay down and laugh as you stretch out in the grass,

And close your eyes in peace and wait for the day to pass.

18.

Limitless

No restrictions. No limits. No bounds.
Just freedom,

Ethereal divine world like the Garden of
Eden,

An endless expanse of the purest form,

From glacial polar ice to aqua
Caribbean warm,

Sapphires and emeralds and
aquamarines,

Deep azure blue to warm forest green,

From calm flat and still on the gentlest of
days,

To tumultuous and tempestuous when
lightning storms blaze,

Dive down deep under the surface and
watch, get lost in the underwater world,

See the creatures and the corals
teaming with vibrance and life and
watch their world unfurl,

Colours that dazzle - reds, oranges and
greens,

Canary yellows and royal blues and
every colour in-between,

Silver flashes of scales dart across the
sea,

And small critters and crabs scuttle over
the sand with glee,

Parrot fish and moray eels and dolphins
and sharks,

These are the creatures with no need
for Noah's ark,

They have been here long before us
and will be here long after we're gone,

Like the ocean's eternal soft breathing,
the tide's song,

Octopi and seahorses and starfish and
shrimp,

Seagrass shades of green growing tall
or hanging limp,

Shipwrecks lie desolate on the ocean
floor,

Once a glorious vessel, alas but no
more,

The sea takes no prisoners, when she
decides she wants you,

Say goodbye to what you know and
love, and bid your life adieu,

Although the ocean takes, she will
always give back,

Unless you're way down deep where the
blue fades to black,

There are so many creatures beneath
the surface down under,

Undisturbed by the clouds, undisturbed
by the thunder,

So much life, so much wonder, so much beauty hidden away,

You never really knew what was buried beneath the waves.

19.

Lost

Frantically running - out of breath and
wild eyed,

Failing to remain calm, freaking out
inside,

Struggling to slow the racing of your
heart,

Dodging and weaving between people
you dart,

There's no one that you recognise -
panic rising in your chest,

As you realise you may not succeed in
your quest,

Heart pounding in your throat, behind
your neck beads of sweat,

Furrowed forehead wrinkles, lines of
fret,

And just as you think that this might be the end,

Come to a skidding halt as you turn the corner round the bend,

See her standing there at the end of the aisle,

Looking at you with a wave and a smile,

With the item in her hand that she'd sent you to find,

You realise now that she would never leave you behind,

She beckons you to her, "Come over here",

"We've got all we need, time to pay the cashier".

20.

Cyber Lust

Sometimes we're too busy in a world of
our own,

And in the age of social media we still
feel alone,

Because no matter if we count on our
picture the number of likes,

In your brand new dress or your shiny
white Nikes,

In the grand scheme of life it really
doesn't matter,

There's silence between the lines of
fake online chatter,

Don't lose sight of what is real and what
is not,

Comparing yourself to others and being
unhappy with your lot,

This online world - it isn't real, it isn't
true,

When all you reveal is only the best bits
of you,

Embrace all you are and all you have
ever been,

Even the bits of you that you've kept
hidden unseen,

Because you are perfect just the way
you are,

You don't have to live up to this false
impossible bar,

Love yourself, who you were, who you
are, who you will be,

Do not blur the lines of stories and
reality.

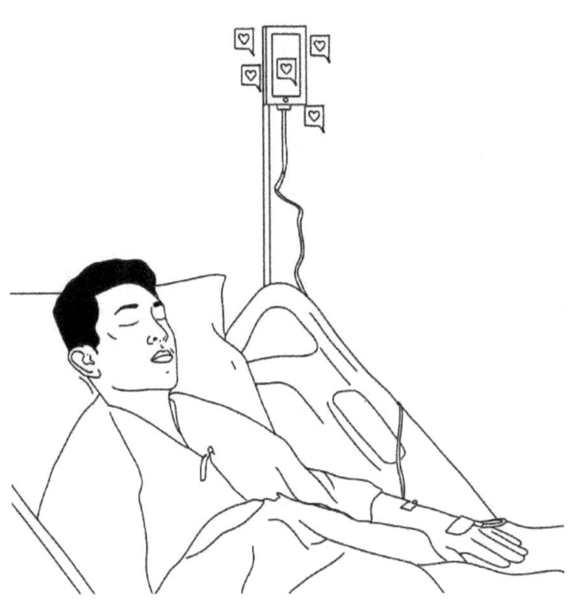